LOVE
AND INSPIRATION
FROM
Mom

LOVING WORDS TO INSPIRE
A HAPPIER YOU

SHELLY SLOCUM

FOREWORD BY **JACK CANFIELD**
CO-AUTHOR OF ***CHICKEN SOUP FOR THE SOUL*** SERIES

This book is not intended to take the place of
professional help. It is critical to seek medical
attention if you or someone you love is facing
a mental health crisis. The author's intent is to
merely provide an inspirational
way of looking at life.

ISBN: 979-8-9859530-0-8

This book was printed in the
United States of America.

Contact info:

www.loveandinspiration.org

Praise for

Love and Inspiration from Mom

"I love this book! The quotes and Shelly's insight and interpretation of each are a thing of beauty. I have read a lot of self-help books and daily inspirationals and this is as good or better than any I have read. Shelly's life outlook is inspiring!"

–Cindy Gotchey

"I believe everyone who reads these treasures of wisdom and daily gems will find joy, hope, and a deep breath of peace like I did!"

–Barb Haines

"This book helped me feel the intricacies and depths of love, from the love of a daughter to the love of one's self. Shelly's interpretation of these meaningful quotes filled a gap in my heart where I've been missing my mom's guidance and encouragement since she passed away. I can't wait to share this treasure with my own daughters!"

–Karen Grimm

Dedicated

*To my wonderful daughters who are
beautiful inside and out.
I couldn't be more proud of the amazing
women you have become.
It is an honor to be your mom!*

Foreword

Love and inspiration are at the heart of a great life! And let's face it, even the strongest among us can use a little more love, especially in the midst of a struggle. Life can be challenging sometimes, and having a place to go for a dose of loving encouragement is a good thing. Shelly Slocum's book, *Love and Inspiration from Mom* is like a warm hug in a book, where she gives practical ways to live a more inspired and happier life from a loving mom.

As the co-author of the highly acclaimed *Chicken Soup for the Soul*® series, I am always on the lookout for books that can make a real difference in people's lives. *Love and Inspiration from Mom* is a gem, and I am excited to see the impact this book has for the readers. I love this book and believe that everyone can benefit from Shelly's wisdom. Words of encouragement and love like these are so needed in our world right now!

When we wrote *Chicken Soup for the Soul*, our mission was to change the world one story at a time. That's the power of *Love and Inspiration from Mom*; together we are making the world a better place one story and one inspired person at a time.

Jack Canfield

Introduction

We have all heard the saying "When life gives you lemons, make lemonade." While this advice sounds like a good idea, we're often at a loss as to how we can actually apply the idea in our daily lives.

As I reflect on the popularity of quote books, quote calendars, inspirational apps, etc., the goal, as I see it, is to read them and feel better, more inspired, and more optimistic. I've found that most people would love to incorporate more positivity and optimism in their lives, but find it difficult to do so when faced with life's many challenges and obstacles. After all, in the midst of a crisis, or when life throws us a curveball, it doesn't seem possible to think about turning our current circumstances into something other than the pain or sadness we are feeling.

Recently, one of my daughters lived through a torturous experience, and as a result of the trauma, she suffered a breakdown. As her mom, I immediately dropped everything in my world and moved to where she lived. Every day for weeks I helped her get out of bed. When she was able to go back to work, I would text her an inspirational quote every morning and add a few tips on how to apply it in her day. Day by day, she got better, stronger, and more optimistic. Soon she was back with an even better outlook on life than before.

I realized, through this experience, that not everyone has someone who can lift them back up. I decided to put those daily encouragements into a book to share with others who might be going through a difficult time.

You see, I have been a self-help, self-improvement junkie my whole life, always buying the latest book to help me solve the questions and challenges of my life. Many have asked me over the years, "Why? Why do you read all of these books and go to all of those conferences and seminars? What is it you think you are going to find?" My only answer to that is perspective.

To me, perspective is anything outside of my head. Left unchecked, the mind can start to make us believe things that simply are not true. Our minds can be very one-sided at times and can warp or skew things. The mind is also very powerful and can be positively influenced as well.

In my quest for learning, I have been blessed to have some amazing mentors, parents, grandparents, teachers, coaches, friends, therapists, my husband and my girls who have helped me navigate life. I have gleaned insights from each, learned both good thoughts and habits to apply in my life, and identified things I would do differently. I had the opportunity to use all of the knowledge I have gained over the years to help my daughter, and now I would like to share those things with you, from a loving mom.

I learned a lot during this difficult time with my daughter, but the most important thing I learned is the Power of Love. Never, ever underestimate the Power of Love: God's love, family love, love from friends, and of course, Mom's love.

It is very important to note that this book is in no way designed to take the place of professional help, which is often necessary when going through challenges. Instead, it is designed to give you another way of looking at things.

So when life gives you lemons, what you need is a plan—a plan for each day to get up, get dressed, and get through the day, putting one foot in front of the other. And you need perspective—something outside of your head to help you see life just a little bit differently.

Use this book however you choose. Some options:

- Read cover to cover at your own pace.
- Read one day at a time in 30-day increments. (This gives you three months to navigate a new, inspired journey.)
- Open the book to a new place each day and trust it's the inspiration and love you need for that day.
- Read through the book three times and benefit from Transformative Learning.[1] The first time through

1 The Head, Heart and Hands Model for Transformative Learning (Orr 1992)

gives some new perspective for your HEAD. The second time gives you an opportunity to apply some or all of the suggestions, giving your HANDS something to do. And the third time through gives you a chance to change your HEART. Let the information flow from your head, to your hands, to your heart.

However you decide to use this book and incorporate the action steps, my prayer is that the love and inspiration will encourage you, uplift you, and make each day a little sweeter.

I have found that the best way to make delicious lemonade is finding the perfect blend of sweet and sour. Life is much the same. Blending the sweetness of good times and growing through the sour times is the perfect recipe for a better life. This book is my family's lemonade for you to SIP and ENJOY!

Love,
Mom

"If you can't fly then run, if you can't run then walk, if you can't walk then crawl, but whatever you do, you have to keep moving forward."

Martin Luther King Jr.

One day you will fly again!
When life takes you out at the
knees, it takes time to rebuild
your strength. Sometimes
you need to go back to the
basics, like getting out of bed
every morning, eating good
healthy meals, and going
outside for fresh air. But don't
be afraid. Our bodies and
minds have muscle memory.
The rebuilding time won't take
as long as it initially took to
learn. You simply must keep
moving every day.

Love,
Mom

"Nothing is impossible, the word itself says I'm possible."

Audrey Hepburn

It's amazing how a tiny shift in how we look at things or think about what's going on can make all the difference in the world. It can be as simple as telling yourself each morning as you get out of bed, "Today I am going to have a better day!" No matter what you are facing, what tiny shift can you make in your thoughts or actions today that reminds you "I'm possible"?

Love,
Mom

"A bird sitting in a tree is never afraid of the branch breaking because its trust is not on the branch but on its own wings."

Author Unknown

Fear erodes the trust we have in ourselves and what we're capable of. Let go of that fear by tapping into who you are at your core, trusting your gut, pushing through what scares you, and doing it anyway. You will amaze yourself with talents, strengths, and abilities that you never knew were in you if you believe in yourself.

Love,
Mom

"Strength does not come from winning. Your struggles develop your strengths. When you go through hardships and decide not to surrender, that is strength."

Arnold Schwarzenegger

The key to this inspiration and in life is to decide. Ultimately, you are in charge of your own white flag. You are the only one who decides when to surrender. Some people are fighters and NEVER give in no matter the circumstances. But for most of us, the longer it takes before you give in, the more you are building strengths to handle the next struggle you face! DECIDE today to be strong and keep fighting.

Love,
Mom

"Learn from yesterday, live for today, hope for tomorrow."

Albert Einstein

If we could apply these three things consistently, every day would be a BETTER day! Yesterday's lessons prepare us for the next obstacles we face. But they're wasted if we don't learn from them and apply our wisdom. Living each day focused on the moment and appreciating each experience as it unfolds is the blessing of the present. And our hopes and dreams for tomorrow allow us to look forward to even brighter days. Every day: Learn, Live, and Hope.

Love,
Mom

"Never be ashamed of a scar. It simply means you were stronger than whatever tried to hurt you."

Author Unknown

External and internal scars are proof that you are stronger than you think! Drawing from the strength you've gained from past pain is an incredible confirmation that you CAN do it again.

Love,
Mom

"When life is sweet, say thank
you and celebrate. And when
life is bitter, say thank
you and grow."

Shauna Niequist

Every challenge we face comes with a lesson. That's why hindsight is 20/20 because we can look back, analyze, and see what we did right and what we would do differently. Jot down the lessons you learn each day in a "Wisdom Journal." Years later, when you look back in your journal, you will likely see that this challenging time was one of the biggest growth spurts you ever had.

Love,
Mom

"Remember that at any given moment there are a thousand things you can love."

David Levithan

When you are sad or in the middle of a struggle, take a minute to change the channel in your mind. Alter the thoughts in your brain, even for just a few minutes, several times a day. Think about things you love and that make you happy. Smile big at the same time! Doing this gives your mind a break and can help shift you into a more positive mindset. Make sure to smile when you are thinking of things you love. You will feel the difference.

Love,
Mom

"I have found that if you love
life, life will love you back."

Arthur Rubinstein

This is a wonderful phenomenon. Many things in life follow this reciprocal, or boomerang, effect. What we give out, we get back. Think of a smile—when we smile, people smile back. Sometimes just making a goal every day to smile, whether you feel like it or not, will help you get momentum and start loving life again, especially when you're rewarded with warm smiles in return. Take the smile challenge today!

Love,
Mom

"Some people come in your life as blessings. Some come in your life as lessons."

Mother Teresa

We can learn something from everyone, whether it is good or bad. Sometimes the most valuable lessons come from the most challenging people. Learn to say, "Thank you for the lesson," and move on.

Love,
Mom

"Don't be pushed by your problems, be led by your dreams."

Proverb

When we are pushed by negative things that happen, we are operating from a place of fear, making us feel out of control. We can get stuck in this vicious, negative cycle. On the flip side, if we allow ourselves to be led by our dreams, we are approaching life from a positive place of hope. With hope, we have things to look forward to, and we can set goals to achieve our dreams. Leading with dreams gives you back a sense of control. Today, make a list of your hopes and dreams, keep it where you can see it, and add something new every day.

Love,
Mom

"Being happy doesn't mean that everything is perfect. It means that you've decided to look beyond the imperfections."

Gerard Way

Many people have a misconception that happiness is all or nothing. The good news is that's simply not true. We can be a little bit happy some days, and we can experience happiness even in sad or difficult times. When you're feeling sad, take a minute to purposefully think about a memory that makes you laugh. Even doing this for a brief time will bring a little happiness and give you a break from life's most challenging imperfections.

Love,
Mom

"When God pushes you to the edge, trust Him fully because only two things will happen. Either He will catch you when you fall or He will teach you how to fly."

Author Unknown

Life is so much better when we have Faith. Trust that there is something bigger than you in charge. So many times when you look back on life's challenges, you will see God's hand guiding you, directing you, and comforting you. Trust in Him.

Love,
Mom

"Accept what is, let go of what was, and have faith in what will be."

Sonia Ricotti

One of the hardest things to
do is letting go of what we
think was supposed to happen,
or what we wish would have
happened. Most of the time,
you will find that things
happen for a reason and help
you become the person you
are meant to be. Sometimes,
accepting "what is" can be
the greatest gift you can
give yourself.

Love,
Mom

"When we stop fighting for
what we want, what we don't
want will automatically
take over."

Les Brown

Life is better when we keep our hands on the steering wheel. Having goals and dreams puts us in the driver's seat of life so we can turn toward what we want. When you take your hands off the wheel and let the car steer itself, you often end up in a place you never intended to go. Fighting for something with great focus allows your body and mind to help you figure out a map to get there.

Love,
Mom

"The best day of your life is the one on which you decide your life is your own.
No apologies or excuses.
No one to lean on, rely on or blame. The gift is yours – it is an amazing journey – and you alone are responsible for the quality of it. This is the day your life really begins."

Bob Moawad

Ultimately, we are responsible
for what we do with our lives.
You can let your injuries,
mistakes, and disappointments
take you down a dark
road of misery and blame,
OR you can decide to use
those things to give you
strength and propel you down
the road you really want to
travel. Let the journey to
your best life begin!

Love,
Mom

"We can let the circumstances
of our lives harden us so
that we become increasingly
resentful and afraid, or we can
let them soften us, and make us
kinder. You always have
the choice."

Dalai Lama

Joy and happiness are difficult to find with a hardened heart. Bitterness, sadness, and negative emotions can build a callus around our heart to protect us, but over time, the callus build up makes it harder and harder for positive emotions to penetrate as well. EVERY day, even in difficult times, look for ways to help others, be kind, and find the good in all circumstances. Doing these things consistently will soften your heart and ultimately help you find joy again.

Love,
Mom

"Remember that the quality of your life is determined by the quality of your thoughts."

Robin Sharma

What we think about and focus on shows up in our life. It is a crazy law of attraction. Whenever you find your mind thinking negatively, STOP and replace it with a positive thought. The more you do this, the better you will get at it, and you will see the quality of your life improve.

Love,
Mom

My to-do list for today:
- Count my blessings
- Practice kindness
- Let go of what I can't control
- Listen to my heart
- Be productive yet calm
- Just breathe

Author Unknown

The most important "To Do" on the list is to start each day with gratitude for all of the blessings in your life. Ask yourself every morning: What am I thankful for today? It can be as simple as "I'm thankful for the sunshine" or "I'm thankful for air to breathe." Beginning with gratitude sets a positive tone for the day so you can accomplish the other important things on your To Do list. If things turn negative at any point in the day, stop and think of something you're grateful for at that moment to help turn things around.

Love,
Mom

"Things work out best for those who make the best of how things work out."

John Wooden

So much of life and how it plays out is what we choose to focus on. It's easy to miss blessings if we are not actively seeking them. Looking for the blessings, big or small, in every situation, will help you make the best of things.

Love,
Mom

"Stars can't shine without darkness."

D.H. Sidebottom

Unfortunately, we can't truly see and appreciate the good things in life without experiencing struggles and pain as well. The good news is that your difficulties will help make the good times shine.

Love,
Mom

"This is the day the Lord has made, we will rejoice and be glad in it."

Psalm 118:24 (NLT)

One of the beautiful aspects of life is that every day God gives us here on this earth, we have the opportunity to make it a better day for ourselves and others. Rejoice in the fact that you have the chance today to love yourself, love others, and do something different if you want to change your current circumstances.

Love,
Mom

"The most difficult thing is the decision to act. The rest is merely tenacity."

Amelia Earhart

Just as it is in physics, it takes a lot more energy to set something into motion than to keep it moving. Once you decide to make a positive change in your life, the hardest part is starting. Make today the day you START and tomorrow, KEEP GOING!

Love,
Mom

"God has planted greatness in you. Let today be the beginning of a great adventure as you step into the gifts He's given you."

Joyce Meyer

Every one of us has untapped potential and talents that we don't use. It's one of life's great tragedies. If we all did the amazing things we are capable of doing, our lives and this world would be incredibly different. Make it a goal to find your hidden talents and start using them.

Love,
Mom

"It's a good day to have a good day!"

Author Unknown

It is amazing how much power we actually have over our mood. Sometimes having a positive mindset in the morning is all we need to start out on a good path. When you wake up, before your feet hit the ground, tell yourself out loud, "Today is going to be a good day!" Do this every morning and your body and mind will go to work to make it happen.

Love,
Mom

"You are confined only by the walls you build yourself."

Andrew Murphy

Many of the obstacles we face in life are ones we put there ourselves because of fear. Small fears turn into big fears when we let them, and they begin to confine us, keep us stuck, and hold us back. This is why you must do something every day that feels scary or outside your comfort zone. Start small, like striking up a conversation with the person next to you in line. Tomorrow, do something a little scarier. Facing fear on purpose builds confidence, erodes anxiety, and tears down your walls brick by brick.

Love,
Mom

"Keep your face to the sunshine
and you cannot see a shadow."

Helen Keller

The sun has wonderful healing powers. Just a few minutes in sunlight warms us and gives us Vitamin D, which is good for our health. Best of all, the sun's brightness helps overcome darkness and shadows.
Every day, go outside, get fresh air, and let the sun work its magic. If you don't have much sunlight where you live, look into getting a light box to mimic some of the sun's benefits.

Love,
Mom

"God, grant me the serenity
to accept the things I cannot
change, courage to change the
things I can, and the wisdom to
know the difference."

Reinhold Niebuhr

One of the biggest mistakes we make is wasting time stressing and worrying about things we have no control over. Worrying gives us something to do, but it doesn't help us solve anything. Instead, pray for God's guidance to see where you CAN make a difference, then put your efforts there.

Love,
Mom

"Stop thinking about what could go wrong and start thinking about what could go right!"

Yoana Dianika

A simple twist in how we choose to look at things gets our mind thinking about the positives instead of the negatives. If you make it a habit of expecting things to go RIGHT, you will find that life is much easier to handle and more enjoyable!

Love,
Mom

"Happiness cannot be traveled to, owned, earned, won or consumed. Happiness is the spiritual experience of living every minute with love, grace and gratitude."

Denis Waitley

One key to unlocking more happiness is finding LITTLE things to be happy about in the moment, all day long. Things that make us smile, laugh, feel tender, feel content—this is happiness. Every time you have one of those happy moments, STOP, acknowledge it, and appreciate the feeling in your body. The more you do this, the more happiness you will find.

Love,
Mom

"Optimism is a happiness magnet. If you stay positive, good things and good people will be drawn to you."

Mary Lou Retton

The opposite is true as well.
Pessimism attracts negative
things and negative people.
If you are going to be magnetic
either way, wouldn't you rather
attract the positive? Life will
be so much better if you look
at the bright side of things and
build your optimism!

Love,
Mom

"I am in charge of how I feel
and today I am choosing
happiness."

Author Unknown

When we finally realize that we are 100% responsible for our own mood, we can start focusing on doing things that will improve it instead of blaming others for how we feel. What is something you can do today that will have a positive effect on your mood and move you in the direction of happiness?

Love,
Mom

"Take pride in how far you
have come and have faith in
how far you can go."

Christian Larson

It is always a good idea to reflect on our improvements and celebrate even the smallest of victories and accomplishments. Reflection and celebration will give you the momentum you need to *keep pushing forward* and achieve even more.

Love,
Mom

"Follow your dreams, they know the way."

Kobi Yamada

It is fascinating how we inherently know what's best for us if we just set aside some quiet time each day to listen to our hearts. Carve out a few minutes each day to sit quietly and ask yourself, "What do I really want?" As you do this, your dreams will become crystal clear.

Love,
Mom

"The first to apologize is the bravest. The first to forgive is the strongest. And the first to forget is the happiest."

Author Unknown

Holding onto grudges and negative feelings is one of the worst things we can do for our health and well-being. Letting anger and resentment fester inside our bodies is like letting weeds take over a garden. The ugly weeds take hold and won't allow the beautiful flowers to grow. The sooner you can apologize, forgive, and forget, the better you will start to feel. Soon, healthy, loving feelings will start to grow again.

Love,
Mom

"He has made everything
beautiful in its time."

Ecclesiastes 3:11 (NKJV)

Patience is the greatest of virtues. We live in a time where instant gratification is what we expect and seek. But few things improve overnight. Take little steps toward your goal every day, and in God's time, He will make life beautiful again!

Love,
Mom

"You hold the key to Happiness. It's your choice to open the door!"

Author Unknown

This is a great way to think about happiness. You do have the Key and it is a Choice! Keep in mind that happiness is not just one door you go through and "*Voilà!*" you're happy. It is a series of doors, thoughts, choices, and decisions throughout your days, weeks, months, and years that lead to a happier life. You never just arrive at happy. Instead, you are always choosing happiness.

Love,
Mom

"You may know me . . . but you have no idea WHO I AM!"

Author Unknown

What people see and know about us on the surface is like the tip of an iceberg. You have more strength and power beneath the surface than you can even imagine. It is exciting to see more and more of your iceberg revealed every day.

Love,
Mom

"Everyone wants happiness. No one wants pain, but you can't make a rainbow without a little rain."

Zion Lee

This is a perfect example
in nature where something
beautiful follows something
difficult. Learn to appreciate
every experience, as challenging
as it may be, knowing that the
rainbow is coming.

Love,
Mom

"She is clothed with strength and dignity, and she laughs without fear of the future."

Proverbs 31:25 (NLT)

Sometimes fear comes from legitimate past experiences, and sometimes it is from things we've built up in our minds over time. One way to stand strong in the grip of fear is to identify its origin and process the chances of whether or not this fear could become a reality, keeping in mind that most of the time, what you fear DOES NOT happen. Then, think about how your future will benefit from getting past the fear and create a mental picture of what life looks like when you move past it. Draw strength from that new picture every time you feel the old fear.

Love,
Mom

"Follow your heart; trust your
wisdom; manage
your thinking."

Jody Stevenson

Unfortunately, we often let our thoughts overrule our gut. We think we KNOW better. But when we consciously start trusting our innate wisdom and following our heart, life gets better and we feel better. Start keeping a log of times when you make a decision to follow your gut instead of what your mind says, and you will begin to see the power of your own wisdom.

Love,
Mom

"Today you are you. That is truer than true. There is no one alive who is you-er than you."

Dr. Seuss

Embrace your You-ness!
Loving and accepting your
unique and special YOU is
a big part of building self-
confidence, which transfers
into living a more fulfilling
and successful life. With more
confidence, you can achieve
more. Today, focus on one
trait you like about yourself.
Tell yourself many times
throughout the day: "I like the
way I _____!" Tomorrow,
add a new trait to acknowledge
and praise yourself. Each day
will build a more confident
and truer YOU!

Love,
Mom

"I've missed more than 9,000 shots in my career. I've lost almost 300 games. 26 times I've been trusted to take the game winning shot and missed. I've failed over and over again in my life. And that is why I succeed."

Michael Jordan

Success comes from
pushing through our misses,
mistakes, and failures.
Remember that you will
NEVER win the game
if you quit. Pushing
through struggles and
disappointments builds the
WINNER in you!

Love,
Mom

"Life is too short to wake up in the morning with regrets. So, love the people who treat you right, forget about those who don't, and believe that everything happens for a reason. If you get the chance, take it. If it changes your life, let it. Nobody said that it would be easy, they just promised it would be worth it."

Harvey Mackay

There is nothing in life more unfulfilling and unproductive than regret. Many people spend their time wishing they would have made different choices that might have changed the course of their lives. This is a WASTE of your time and energy! Commit to letting go of those "wish I would have," "wish I could have," thoughts and trust that you made the best decision you could with the information you had at the time. Start living a life of NO regrets.

Love,
Mom

"If information alone could change people, everyone would be skinny, rich and happy."

Les Brown

For the most part, knowledge is not enough. Simply knowing what we need to do will never get us where we want to go. We MUST DO SOMETHING. Until you take action and start to put what you KNOW to work, you will stay stuck in the rut of wishing and hoping that things will change. Make today a DO-day!

Love,
Mom

"The best way out is
always through!"

Robert Frost

As much as we would love
to avoid difficulties in life,
hard things will come, and
usually when we least expect
them. The emotional and
physical recovery time from
struggle will be much quicker
the sooner you start. What
step can you take today to
start moving through the
pain toward healing? Is it
counseling, rehabilitation,
finding a support group,
talking to a minister?
Whatever it is, do something
today to help move you
forward and through
this challenge.

Love,
Mom

"Helping others is the way we help ourselves."

Oprah Winfrey

When bad things happen, there is no question that it is important to grieve, mourn, be sad, process, and reflect. Once you have taken the time you need for yourself to heal, the very best way to get back into life is to help someone else.

Love,
Mom

"Believe you can and you're halfway there."

Theodore Roosevelt

The power of belief is very strong. Believing in ourselves, believing in our potential, and believing "Why not me?" is how we start toward achieving any goal. The very first step in doing anything is getting your mind on board. Your mind directs your body, so if your mind believes you can, it will put your body in motion. Belief is powerful. What the mind believes, it will help you achieve.

Love,
Mom

"Life is like a camera. Focus on what's important. Capture the good time. And if things don't work out, take another shot."

Ziad K. Abdelnour

This quote captures what having a good life is all about. Too often, we focus on the negative instead of the positive. We remember the bad instead of the good. This keeps us stuck and afraid to try again. Don't let that happen anymore. Start looking at the world as if through a camera, focus on what you want, keep only the good pictures in your mind, and give your dreams another shot.

Love,
Mom

"The only person you should try to be better than is the person you were yesterday."

Matty Mullins

This is great advice. If you can get just a little bit better each and every day—better attitude, better outlook, better knowledge, better approach— just imagine how amazing you will be.

Love,
Mom

"I'm thankful for my struggle
because without it, I wouldn't
have stumbled across
my strength."

Alex Elle

Just like a butterfly goes through the struggles and stages from caterpillar to chrysalis and finally to a beautiful butterfly, every process has its challenges. Remember that every step along the way is building strength in you for the next hurdle.

Love,
Mom

"Don't allow your wounds to transform you into someone you are not."

Paulo Coelho

If we allow bad things or circumstances to change the essence of who we are, we run the risk of not being the person God intended us to be. Our wounds are best used to teach us how to be better and stronger. Use each experience in life to become a better version of you.

Love,
Mom

"Feelings are much like waves,
we can't stop them from
coming but we can choose
which ones to surf."

Jonatan Mårtensson

Even though we don't get to control a lot of things in our life, we definitely don't have to stay with every emotion and feeling that comes our way. Acknowledge the emotion you are experiencing and ask yourself if continuing to feel this way is serving you well. If it isn't, choose another emotion.

Love,
Mom

"What lies behind us and what lies before us are tiny matters compared to what lies within us."

Ralph Waldo Emerson

Believe it or not, you have what it takes inside you right now to be and do whatever you choose. Tap into your God-given abilities and you will be unstoppable.

Love,
Mom

"Without hard work, nothing grows but weeds."

Gordon B. Hinckley

Gardening is HARD work and requires daily attention tending to and caring for the precious crop. Yet surprisingly, the weeds grow with absolutely no effort at all. In general, life is much the same. Bad habits seem to take over with little effort, and good, successful habits are hard to form and stick to. Without hard work and good habits, true and lasting success will not come. When you tend to your life like you tend to a garden, working hard and giving it your all every day, you will harvest many rewards from your efforts.

Love,
Mom

"God can restore what is broken and change it into something amazing. All you need is faith."

Author Unknown

It is amazing to watch
God's work. Just look at the
devastation from a forest fire
where everything in sight
is black and charred, yet
eventually, green grass begins
to sprout and trees start to
grow again, ever so slowly but
surely. TRUST that God can
and will do the same thing
in your life.

Love,
Mom

"Every path has its puddle."

English Proverb

As much as we would love for everything in life to be rosy, we know that our lives will never be ALL good. One trick to life is looking at it like a path, enjoying the views as you walk, trusting that when you get through the puddles you will be on the path again.

Love,
Mom

"Every test in life makes us bitter or better, every problem comes to break us or make us. The choice is ours whether we become victim or victor."

Author Unknown

One way to help turn the tide in challenging times and become better and stronger is to change your questions from Why's to What's. Instead of asking: "Why me? Why now? Why this?" Change your questions to: "What can I learn from this? What can I do to make things better? What can I change?" Asking questions that help you focus on what you CAN do will help you become a victor over your circumstances.

Love,
Mom

"If you do what is easy, your life will be hard. If you do what is hard, your life will be easy."

Les Brown

We all wish we could take the easy road, use the quick fix, or put in the least amount of effort to get where we want to go. Unfortunately, the best things in life never come easy. There is ALWAYS a price to pay through hard work, patience, and perseverance. But when you put in the time and effort, the rewards are far greater and your life will be easier in the long run.

Love,
Mom

"When writing the story of
your life, don't let anyone
else hold the pen."

Harley Davidson

When limiting thoughts and beliefs surface in our lives, it's important to realize that many of them have been written into our minds from others through criticism, shame, and discouragement. One way to take the pen back from whoever or whatever has written in your life story is to question your thoughts. Ask yourself: "Where did this belief come from, and is it helping me or hurting me?" Pick up that pen. You can start today, writing a new chapter in the story of a life you can be proud of.

Love,
Mom

"Keep your thoughts positive because your thoughts become your words. Keep your words positive because your words become your behavior. Keep your behavior positive because your behavior becomes your habits. Keep your habits positive because your habits become your values. Keep your values positive because they become your destiny."

Mahatma Gandhi

Your destiny begins with you and your thoughts! Start thinking positive thoughts today, keep it up every day, and you will be destined for greatness.

Love,
Mom

"Don't wait for the perfect moment, take the moment and make it perfect."

Zoey Sayward

Too many times, we let opportunities and life pass us by because we are waiting for the right time. How will you ever know until you try? Stop waiting. Take action now! Whatever it is you have been longing to do, START today. There couldn't be a more perfect time.

Love,
Mom

"Be happy, not because everything is good, but because you can see the good in everything!"

Author Unknown

Looking for the silver lining in everything is a good idea, and it can make us happier.
Too often, we remember all of the bad things from a situation. Life is so much better if you look for the good and for the lessons and blessings in every event. Even bad experiences can have tiny, hidden blessings if you remember to look for them.

Love,
Mom

"Character cannot be developed in ease and quiet. Only through experience of trial and suffering can the soul be strengthened, vision cleared, ambition inspired and success achieved. It is in the most trying times that our real character is shaped and revealed."

Helen Keller

We are like steel and glass. Both materials are vulnerable and strong, depending on their state. When steel and glass are heated, they can be molded into amazing and beautiful things. Think of life as a series of heating up and cooling off that helps mold and strengthen you, and NEVER waste an opportunity to smooth off your rough edges!

Love,
Mom

"People become attached to
their burdens sometimes more
than the burdens are
attached to them."

George Bernard Shaw

Sometimes we let our past pain become a crutch that we use as an excuse. It can feel easier to stay in self-pity than to stand up again and take charge of our life and thoughts. Make a commitment to yourself that you are done with the pity party. Your pain will no longer be an anchor holding you down. Instead, let your pain drive you to make things better. The past does not have a grip on you.

Love,
Mom

"I am always doing what I cannot do yet, in order to learn how to do it."

Vincent van Gogh

Many times we avoid starting something new because of fear that we won't be good at it, or because we're afraid of what others might think. But the truth is, it's in learning new things that we grow and expand our comfort zones. I challenge you to pick a skill or task that you would love to learn, and push yourself to do something every day that helps you learn how to do it: get books, take lessons, and practice. You will be amazed at what you can learn and master.

Love,
Mom

"Call it a clan, call it a network, call it a tribe, call it a family. Whatever you call it, whoever you are, you need one."

Jane Howard

We were meant to do life with others. If left alone for too long we become depressed, withdrawn, sad, and discouraged. The more isolated we are, the lonelier we become. Being alone is not healthy and definitely not how we were designed to live. Every day, get out and interact with others. Join a club, start a club, take a class. Whatever you decide to do, get yourself around people.

Love,
Mom

"Talk to yourself like you would to someone you love!"

Brené Brown

Sadly, most of us say very mean things to ourselves in self-talk. We say things we would never say to anyone else. One step in turning things around in life is becoming aware of what you're telling yourself. When you catch yourself saying something mean in your head, stop mid-sentence and replace the words with encouragement instead. Say things like "I CAN do this," "I AM stronger than I think," "I'm almost there," "I WILL survive!" By giving yourself these positive pep talks repeatedly, your mind will start to feel the love, and your self-talk will become more kind.

Love,
Mom

"Positive thinking evokes more energy, more initiative, more happiness."

Author Unknown

Happy people think positively. Catch yourself when you're thinking negative thoughts. Stop and ask yourself, "How can I turn these thoughts around and look at this from a positive perspective? What is good about this situation?" Even if you only find a tiny sliver of good, this practice will start to train your brain to look for positives instead of negatives. Do this every time you think negatively and you will be surprised how much happier you become.

Love,
Mom

"The mind is everything. What you think, you become."

Gautama Buddha

The mind is more powerful
than we think, and it is
like a sponge, absorbing
everything we see and hear.
For this reason, be careful
what you listen to and watch.
If it isn't something you want
permanently in your brain,
change the channel and save
yourself future grief.

Love,
Mom

"The grass is greener where
you water it."

Neil Barringham

While there is truth in this, and things that are cared for typically grow, don't get caught up in the comparison game, especially in this messy social media world. It's easy to believe what we see in posts, thinking that everyone else's lives are better than ours. Remember, it is also true that the grass is greener when someone paints it green. What you are seeing through the screen may be an illusion and not green at all.

Love,
Mom

"Start by doing what's necessary; then do what's possible; and suddenly you are doing the impossible."

Saint Francis of Assisi

A wise person once told me, "When facing life's storms, stay vertical!" Getting vertical is necessary. In a crisis, our tendency is to go horizontal. We curl inward in the fetal position and sleep in an attempt to protect ourselves. Staying vertical, as much as possible, gets you up, opens your heart and breath, and keeps you connected to God and life. Before you know it, you will be doing what may seem impossible right now.

Love,
Mom

"We tend to forget that happiness doesn't come as a result of getting something we don't have, but rather recognizing and appreciating what we do have."

Friedrich Koenig

We waste a lot of good life yearning for that elusive joyful day, thinking that we will finally be happy once something big happens. Instead, we should think of happiness like a muscle. We can build our happiness with consistent exercises, like being thankful for the little things we already have and finding joy in THIS moment. Build your happiness muscles and you will appreciate the results.

Love,
Mom

"Gratitude is the open door
to abundance."

Author Unknown

Living life with a scarcity mindset is like living in a room full of closed doors. Our movement and vision are limited to what we can see. On the contrary, living life with gratitude is what opens those doors to an abundant life. Scarcity comes from a place of fear and limits, while abundance comes from a place of gratitude and joy. Let gratitude begin to open your doors to abundance.

Love,
Mom

"The cure for boredom is curiosity. There is no cure for curiosity."

Dorothy Parker

Remember how learning new things was so exciting when we were kids? Then, as we got older, we started to think we knew so much and stopped being curious. We stopped questioning how and why things are the way they are. Bring back your sense of wonder and start being curious about life again. You will be surprised by how much you learn and you'll never be bored again.

Love,
Mom

"We have to learn to be our own best friend because we fall too easily into the trap of being our own worst enemy."

Roderick Thorp

Our thoughts can be encouraging and motivating, or they can be discouraging and take the wind out of our sails. Listen intently to what you tell yourself and ask, "Is this friend or foe? Would I say this to my best friend?" If not, stop talking!

Love,
Mom

"God gives us dreams a size too
big so that we can grow
into them."

Author Unknown

Playing it small when we only have one life to live is a mistake. Have BIG dreams and goals in your life—they are God's gift to you, and achieving them is your loving gift to Him!

Love,
Mom

"For every reason it's not possible, there are hundreds of people who have faced the same circumstances and succeeded."

Jack Canfield

Isn't it amazing how two people can experience a similar illness, accident, or tragedy, and one becomes miserable and depressed, and the other uses the experience to become a better person? The difference can come from many things: support, attitude, faith. But when you stand at the crossroad of misery or success—YOU pick!

Love,
Mom

"The constitution only gives people the right to pursue happiness. You have to catch it yourself."

Benjamin Franklin

Seeking happiness is not a passive sport where you sit back and wait to be happy. Happiness does not pursue you; you must pursue it.

Love,
Mom

"Never measure the height
of a mountain until you have
reached the top."

Dag Hammarskjöld

When starting out, our goals often seem bigger and more overwhelming than they actually are. It's a good idea to begin by writing out the goal, having a detailed picture in your mind of what it will look like when you achieve it. Then start taking daily steps to get there. Don't let the big picture overwhelm you. Today, you only have to take the first step toward the goal, and tomorrow, take the next. If you do something every day, before you know it you will have an amazing view from the top of your mountain.

Love,
Mom

"Where the road bends
abruptly, take short steps."

Ernest Bramah

Even when we think we're on the right path, there are always obstacles and unexpected changes that come up and have the potential to derail our progress. Spending time each morning praying, thinking, planning, and evaluating your goals will help you make small adjustments, if needed, and figure out the next best steps to take.

Love,
Mom

"In seed time learn, in harvest teach, in winter enjoy."

William Blake

There is an important sequence in all of nature that transfers to our lives as well. Unfortunately, we have developed a microwave mentality that falsely leads us to believe we can bypass the important steps and end up with what we want NOW! Don't fool yourself; shortcuts to anything worth having ALWAYS fall short!

Love,
Mom

"When the winds of change blow, some people build walls and others build windmills."

Chinese Proverb

God designed us to live
and grow. Our lifecycle
demonstrates this design,
starting as newborns and
growing old. Change is a
given, don't fight it; embrace
it. Learn to be more flexible
and less rigid as you grow and
change. Look for something to
love about the process or the
result of changing. Hanging
onto the past or the status quo
will not bring you happiness;
it will only hold you
back from experiencing
the fullness of life.

Love,
Mom

"A great pleasure in life is
doing what people say
you cannot do."

Walter Bagehot

There is something powerful in the words "I'll show you!" Whether it's proving to someone else or proving to ourselves that we CAN and WILL do something is the greatest feeling. Don't let doubts creep in when you set your mind to accomplish your dreams. Keep that "I'll show you" attitude, and soon you will show yourself and the world the incredible things you are capable of.

Love,
Mom

"One way to get the most out
of life is to look upon it
as an adventure."

William Feather

While it is very important to have good habits in life, doing the same thing day in and day out can get boring, unfulfilling, and lead you to questioning, "Is this all there is?" Sprinkle in mini get-aways, big vacations, attend a museum, concert, the zoo, or simply try a new restaurant. Having exciting experiences to look forward to, trying new things, and planning fun adventures adds the spice in life you need.

Love,
Mom

"Persistence overshadows even talent as the most valuable resource shaping the quality of life."

Tony Robbins

Once you decide on your new
path and goals,
become tenacious about
achieving them.
If you need help staying on
track, which most of us do,
find an accountability partner
to help you persist. We can
often let ourselves off the hook
and justify why we couldn't get
something done, but a good
accountability partner will not
accept excuses.

Love,
Mom

"A comfort zone is meant to rest and recover and to be of comfort. It's not meant to be a permanent state."

Brian Buffini

Being comfortable should never be the goal. We should spend part of each day growing and expanding our comfort zone because beautiful life exists outside of it. Becoming complacent and staying in what "feels" comfortable now will soon become a type of self-imposed barrier holding you back from learning, experiencing, and growing. Life is best when you are growing. Make it your goal to do something that feels uncomfortable today.

Love,
Mom

"A well developed sense of humor is the pole that adds balance to your steps as you walk the tight rope of life."

William Arthur Ward

Humor and laughter are one of the secrets to a happy life. When navigating the treacherous waters we face, we must take every opportunity we can find to be lighthearted and laugh! Instead of watching TV shows or movies that add more darkness, watch comedies instead. Find the humor in life and laugh out loud when you do. It will be good for your soul.

Love,
Mom

"People will hate you, rate you, shake you and break you. But how strong you stand is what makes you."

Author Unknown

In this world of quick to judge, no grace for people who think differently, and lack of concern for others, we are creating a culture of fear and anxiety. Don't fall into the trap! Love is the answer no matter the question. Lean into your faith, find commonness instead of differences, be kind, be open to others' ideas, listen more, speak less, and ALWAYS lead with LOVE!

Love,
Mom

"Some of it's magic, and some of it's tragic, but I had a good life all the way."

Jimmy Buffett

Life has a way of giving us many ups and downs and twists and turns. It is certainly not possible to have everything figured out. And just when we think we might, another challenging opportunity to learn and grow comes our way. That's the beauty of life, and I'm learning that along with you. Hold on through the tragic, enjoy the magic, and choose to MAKE it a GOOD life all the way!

Love,
Mom

About the Author

Shelly Slocum has been a real estate broker for over twenty years and an instructor for Dale Carnegie Training. But she believes her most important job has been as a mother to her two wonderful daughters! She is now savoring the ultimate reward of parenting - being MiMi to three grandchildren. She and her high school sweetheart enjoy life together in their native state of Colorado.

As a non-smoking lung cancer survivor, Shelly believes she has been given the gift of time and has made it her mission to spread more love and inspiration in the world. To connect with Shelly, please visit her website: www.loveandinspiration.org

A portion of all book proceeds will be donated to *The Imagine Project, Inc.* which gives kids the tools to overcome the stress, trauma and drama of everyday life.

www.ingramcontent.com/pod-product-compliance
Lightning Source LLC
Chambersburg PA
CBHW070703130626
46553CB00005B/1809